Migrating Animals of the Air

by Jacqueline A. Ball

Reading consultant:

Susan Nations, M.Ed.

author, literacy coach, and consultant in literacy development

Science and curriculum consultant:

Debra Voege, M.A.

science and math curriculum resource teacher

WEEKLY READER

PUBLISHING

Please visit our web site at: www.garethstevens.com
For a free color catalog describing our list of high-quality books,
call 1-800-542-2595 (USA) or 1-800-387-3178 (Canada).

Library of Congress Cataloging-in-Publication Data available upon request from publisher.

ISBN-13: 978-0-8368-8417-3 (lib. bdg.)
ISBN-10: 0-8368-8417-5 (lib. bdg.)
ISBN-13: 978-0-8368-8422-7 (softcover)
ISBN-10: 0-8368-8422-1 (softcover)

This edition first published in 2008 by
Weekly Reader® Books
An imprint of Gareth Stevens Publishing
1 Reader's Digest Road
Pleasantville, NY 10570-7000 USA

Copyright © 2008 by Gareth Stevens, Inc.

Photo credits: Cover: © Photodisc/Business & Industry, Vol.1; p.4-21: © Photodisc/Techno
Finance; cover: © www.operationmigration.org; p.5: Eric and David Hosking/Corbis; p.6:
Masterfile; p.8: Digital Vision/Getty, Tom Vezo/Minden Pictures; p.11: AP Images; p.14:
Tim Laman/Getty Images; p.15: Dr. Merlin D Tuttle/Photo Researchers; p.20, 21: Maresa Pryor/
Animals Animals

Printed in the United States of America

1 2 3 4 5 6 7 8 9 11 10 09 08 07

Table of Contents

Cover and title page: Whooping cranes save energy as they fly by gliding on wind currents.

Why Do Animals Migrate?

Long ago, people in a village in England tried to solve a mystery. Most of the birds in the village disappeared every winter and returned in the spring. Where did they go? Someone came up with an answer: The birds must be hiding underwater in the frozen lakes.

Today we know the truth. Birds and other animals leave home in a movement called **migration**. Migration is a regular journey from one place to another. Animals migrate to find food or escape enemies. They migrate to reproduce or to find more comfortable weather. Some animals need to be in a warm climate year-round, so they move as the seasons change. Many animals make round-trip journeys, spending part of a year in one place, part in another.

Migrating birds stop along the way at ponds, lakes, and rivers.

Chapter 1

Birds on the Wing

Every autumn, billions of northern birds get on the move. The insects, caterpillars, and fruits they eat become scarce as the weather grows colder. In the warmer south, there's plenty to eat. The birds take to the air in huge flocks and begin to fly south.

Forests of the Northern Hemisphere are home to billions of birds.

Scientists think less daylight or the change in the weather sets off an **internal clock** inside the birds. It signals that it is time to leave.

Before flying south, birds eat a lot to fatten up. Some small birds double their body weight. They need the energy for the long trip ahead. Many birds fly long distances to reach their winter homes. The arctic tern holds the record. It travels about 22,000 miles (35,400 km) from the **Arctic Circle** to the edge of Antarctica and back again.

Migration Route of Arctic Tern

KEY

Birds Fly South in the Autumn

Birds Fly North in the Spring

7

Many birds rest along their route, but not all get the chance. The tiny ruby-throated hummingbird flies for 30 hours straight across the Gulf of Mexico. The blackpoll warbler flies up to 90 hours across the Atlantic Ocean. These birds travel across the water with no stops for food, water, or rest. Both tiny travelers wait to take off until the wind is coming from behind them. The **tailwind** helps push them along.

The tiny ruby-throated hummingbird weighs very little but flies non-stop at about 30 miles (48 km) an hour across the Gulf of Mexico to its winter home.

The skies are busy day and night during migration times. Small birds like warblers fly at night to hide from their enemies. Some birds fly almost 5 miles (8 km) high! Hawks and eagles fly by day to take advantage of rising columns of air that have been warmed by the daytime sun. The currents of warm air allow them to soar and glide and save energy.

A trip can take several weeks or several months.

The blackpoll warbler flies about 3,000 miles (4,800 km). It burns less than an ounce of fat for fuel for the entire trip!

Chapter 2

Clouds of Insects

Insects migrate for the same purposes as birds. Some insects also move to find more space for their huge **colonies**, or groups. Some insects navigate, as birds do. Many, however, are simply swept up into swarms and blown by the wind. They make new homes wherever they land. Almost all insects are one-way travelers. They don't live long enough to make a return trip.

The African desert locust is a champion long-distance insect. It needs to find a dry place to reproduce, so during the rainy season it takes off on its migration. Some locusts have turned up 2,800 miles (4,506 km) away from their northern Africa homes; they have been found on islands in the Caribbean! Sometimes locusts migrate alone, but sometimes they migrate in huge groups. So many of them may fill the sky that they look like a black cloud. Migrating locusts can cause huge damage to crops when they land in their new territory.

They can eat so many plants so fast that after they pass by, the area looks as if a giant lawnmower cut down everything in its path.

At least 25 kinds of dragonflies migrate. One is the green darner. Like all flying insects, green darners travel during the day. But like birds, green darners wait until strong winds die down before taking off. Scientists think the dragonfly's huge eyes help it navigate.

A thick cloud of locusts eats away at this desert tree.

Monarch butterflies have beautiful orange and black wings. Many monarchs spend spring and summer months near the West Coast of the United States, across much of the eastern United States, and in Canada. As butterflies, most monarchs have a short life of two to six weeks. They spend most of this time mating and laying eggs for a new generation.

Monarch butterflies that hatch at the end of the summer, however, behave differently. They do not mate or lay eggs. Instead they migrate hundreds, or even thousands, of miles or kilometers south. They gather by the millions in the cold mountains of Mexico. There they cling to the branches and trunks of trees. Their body processes slow down. They live off fat stored in their bodies.

Monarchs cluster on the trunk and branches of a tree to rest.

In the spring they begin to "wake up." They mate and lay eggs. They prepare for the journey north. Most of the monarchs that begin the long journey get only halfway "home." They die along the way. Some of their offspring complete the journey.

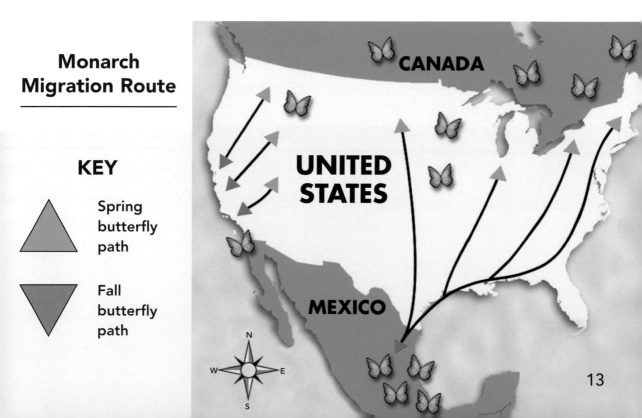

Monarch Migration Route

KEY

△ Spring butterfly path

▽ Fall butterfly path

CANADA

UNITED STATES

MEXICO

Chapter 3

Bats With Wings and Wingless Things

Not just insects and birds migrate by air. One kind of flying mammal does—the bat. The Mexican free-tailed bat travels from Oregon to southern Mexico every winter. A free-tailed bat can cover about 37 miles (60 km) a night.

The nectar bat migrates up to 1,000 miles (1,600 km) from its summer **roost**, looking for a place where its favorite plants are flowering and full of sweet nectar.

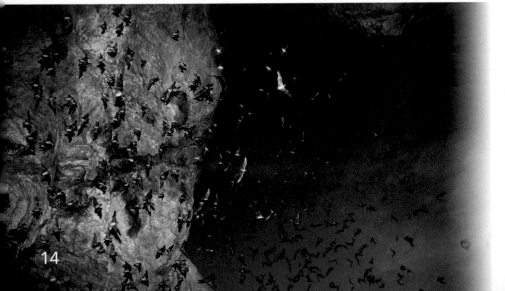

Bats swarm out of caves at dusk.

Nectar bats are attracted to the nectar of many cactus plants.

For some creatures, wings are not necessary to migrate by air. Newly hatched spiders, called **spiderlings**, swing through the air on silk threads spun from their **abdomens**. The breeze catches the threads and carries them off. That type of migration is called **ballooning**. It can carry spiders many miles, even out to sea. Ballooning spiders have been found more than 60 miles (100 kilometers) off shore.

Spiderling Gets Ready To Balloon

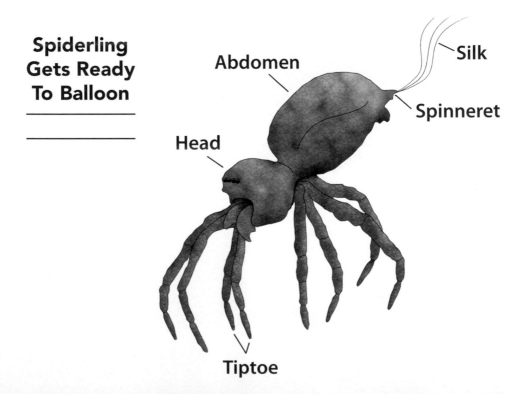

Abdomen

Silk

Spinneret

Head

Tiptoe

Chapter 4

Dangers of Migration

Migrating animals face many dangers. Butterflies can be blasted by storms. Natural enemies are everywhere. Humans have damaged or changed migration routes and resting places with their buildings and roads. Birds and bats might crash into windows, radio towers, and wind turbines.

Scientists and other concerned people are trying to help migratory animals. Preserving their routes and resting places helps preserve the animals themselves.

The first step for scientists is to learn as much as they can about how and where animals migrate. To track butterflies, scientists attach tiny paper tags to their wings. These tags have a telephone number people can call if they find a tagged butterfly. People report the butterfly's location. That helps scientists track migration routes and find where home ranges are. Sometimes scientists attach radio **transmitters** to insects and birds. The transmitters send out signals. To track a green darner, scientists glue on a transmitter that is one-third the weight of a paper clip.

The transmitters send a signal that gets picked up by tracking instruments. On a screen, observers can see birds, insects, migration routes, and traveling speeds. Scientists can even identify different types of birds by the patterns made by their flapping wings.

Sometimes animals need extra-special help. Not many **whooping cranes** are left in the world. A flock of about 200 wild cranes flies south to Texas from the Canadian north every year. Other whooping cranes have been raised in captivity in Wisconsin. Scientists wanted to start a new migrating group that would winter in Florida. They worked with some cranes raised in captivity. But there was a problem. There were no older cranes that had made the journey. Young cranes learn migration routes by following experienced birds.

Scientists track migrating butterflies by attaching tiny paper tags to them.

Pilots William Lishman and Joe Duff had a solution. They would teach young cranes to fly behind **ultralight aircraft**. Then they would lead the birds from their summer home in Wisconsin to their winter home in Florida. They hoped the birds would learn the route as they went.

The plan worked. Since 2001, the pilots trained about 18 cranes a year to "follow the leader." The birds learned to follow a lightweight plane as it flew slowly across the landscape. They led the flock from Wisconsin to Florida. The hope is that over time, birds trained with ultralight aircraft will learn to follow migration routes on their own.

Follow the leader: young cranes learned to follow ultra light aircraft in a migration from Wisconsin to Florida.

Spotlight: Operation Migration

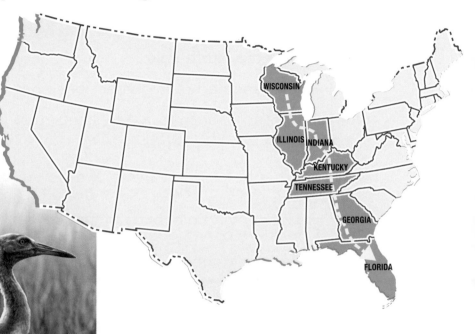

WISCONSIN

ILLINOIS INDIANA

KENTUCKY

TENNESSEE

GEORGIA

FLORIDA

The pilots of Operation Migration teach young whooping cranes to follow ultralight aircraft. The ultralight aircraft leads a new group of young cranes on a soaring, gliding flight from Wisconsin to Florida every year. By 2007, 55 "whoopers" were making the round trip on their own.

Glossary

abdomen—in a spider, where the silk-producing organs are found

Arctic Circle—an imaginary line that marks the region surrounding the North Pole

ballooning—a method of migration for spiders

colony—a group of animals, such as ants, that live together and depend on one another

home range—the place an animal lives for an extended period of time

internal clock—a brain signal that tells an animal when to eat, sleep, migrate, and so on

migration—a regular journey from one place to another to find food, to mate, or to find a better climate

navigate—to find a way to a place

process—a natural body activity, such as breathing

roost—a place where bats or birds gather

spiderling—a newly hatched spider

tailwind—a wind going in the same direction as a traveler

transmitter—a device that gives off a signal

ultralight aircraft—a one-person airplane that runs on a small, gasoline engine

wind turbine—a tall tower with blades to catch wind and generate electricity

For More Information

Books

The Boy Who Drew Birds: A Story of John James Audubon, Jacqueline Davies. (Houghton-Mifflin)

The Journey: Stories of Migration, Cynthia Rylant. (Blue Sky Press)

Birds in Fall, Steve Maslowski. (Smart Apple Media)

Web Sites

www.nationalzoo.si.edu/ConservationAndScience/MigratoryBirds/

www.birding.about.com/od/allaboutbirds/Bird_Facts_and_Information.htm

www.audubon.org/bird/

Index

About the Author

Jacqueline A. Ball has written more than 100 books for kids and teenagers. Her book, *Which Came First: Food Creations,* was named a 2006 Children's Choice winner. *National Geographic Investigates: Ancient China*, which she coauthored, was the lead title in a series that *Booklist* magazine named one of its Top Ten Nonfiction Series for Youth in 2007. She lives in New York City near Central Park, which is visited every year by up to 250 kinds of birds on their annual migration.